THE DIVINE VOLUMES OF
POWER

ROXANNE SAINT-MARIE

BALBOA.
PRESS

A DIVISION OF HAY HOUSE

Balboa Press books may be ordered through booksellers or by contacting:

Balboa Press
A Division of Hay House
1663 Liberty Drive
Bloomington, IN 47403
www.balboapress.com
1 (877) 407-4847

Because of the dynamic nature of the Internet, any web addresses or links contained in this book may have changed since publication and may no longer be valid. The views expressed in this work are solely those of the author and do not necessarily reflect the views of the publisher, and the publisher hereby disclaims any responsibility for them.

The author of this book does not dispense medical advice or prescribe the use of any technique as a form of treatment for physical, emotional, or medical problems without the advice of a physician, either directly or indirectly. The intent of the author is only to offer information of a general nature to help you in your quest for emotional and spiritual well-being. In the event you use any of the information in this book for yourself, which is your constitutional right, the author and the publisher assume no responsibility for your actions.

Any people depicted in stock imagery provided by Getty Images are models, and such images are being used for illustrative purposes only. Certain stock imagery © Getty Images.

Print information available on the last page.

ISBN: 978-1-9822-2153-9 (sc)
ISBN: 978-1-9822-2152-2 (hc)
ISBN: 978-1-9822-2154-6 (e)

Library of Congress Control Number: 2019901488

Balboa Press rev. date: 02/08/2019

CONTENTS

ACKNOWLEDGMENTS

I would like to acknowledge my husband who inspired and supported me in completing my soul purpose by writing this book. The ancient wisdom he shared with me led me on a path of spiritual development; his divine love and devotion encouraged me through all my moments of uncertainty, and for that, I am forever grateful to him.

To my greatest teacher of all, my mother, who taught me the love of Christ, Mother Mary and The Archangels. She took me to museums and symphonies and initiated my love for history and the arts at an early age. She provided an abundant childhood filled with love, excitement, and wonder.

I would like to honor my angel in heaven, my ascended family member, my sister, who would give the shirt off her back to someone in need. Her giving heart taught me to give to those in need. She was one of my greatest teachers in life. She always said, "You never know, that homeless man could be an angel." She taught me to give and be selfless and to never place judgment on others.

To all those who have touched my life and supported me, I am humbled by your loving energy. May your light continue to shine ever so bright.

INTRODUCTION

In everyday life, we experience conflicting events. We experience anger, pain, stress, and many other negative emotions. A human's life can be burdened while operating with this instinctive or primitive mind-set, but it does not have to be this way. God has provided us with a way—a holy way—to relieve ourselves of the negative emotions we encounter throughout our lives. Contrary to some people's beliefs, we are not alone in the universe. God created divine beings (angels) and various forms of healing to aid us in our times of need.

Some of us do not know of their existence, and some of us doubt their existence altogether. But whether we choose to believe it or not, they do exist.

People experience recurring cycles of pain or misfortune because they have yet to connect with God and the kingdom of heaven. When you connect to the heavens, you allow blessings, knowledge, and abundance to enter your life. You obtain the knowledge and wisdom to understand that everything is in divine order. You establish this by learning to let go, give it to God, and have faith. Master the art of letting go by giving it to God and you will find peace.

We all have intentions and desires, and in this book, you will gain insight into how to attain these in a spiritually pure way.

In this book, I lead you on a journey that teaches you how obtain and utilize the power of the divine.

When God created the universe, he created various resources for the benefit of our physical and spiritual bodies, both visible and invisible to the human eye. We have everything necessary to nourish and protect our physical and spiritual wellbeing.

In this book, I lift the veil and reveal the powerful abilities God has gifted to us. I explain the power of intention, the power of touch, the power of gratitude, and the power of kindness, which is by far my favorite.

In this book, I share my own spiritual routines for connecting to God and the heavens.

God's infinite blessings are waiting for you. Ask and you shall receive. Knock and the door shall open.

My intention is to share this knowledge with you, and the wisdom to apply it. Once you embark on this sacred, eye-opening journey, you will feel compelled to share it with your loved ones. Rest assured, once you practice the teachings in this book, you will begin to feel a positive shift in your vibration that all others will sense and be attracted to. All of God's creation depends on the light to grow. In fact, we gravitate to it. That's why you are here now, reading this very introduction. Many blessings be upon you this day.

Enjoy, and remember, practice makes perfect!

CHAPTER 1
POWERFUL ROUTINES

When seeking a powerful routine, one

must seek the highest vibration that

brings inspiration and motivation,

thus resulting in infinite creation.

The most significant element of this book is going to be shared with you in the coming pages. I intended powerful routines to be the initiating part of this enlightened journey, solely to validate its virtue. It is that powerful and significant!

Before we get started, first and foremost I will begin by saying thank you. I am truly honored to share my experience with you and what I believe is powerful, life-changing, spiritual knowledge. I am thankful that you possess an open heart and mind to the endless possibilities, and allow me to plant a seed of divine love, good works, and spiritual awareness into the depths of your mind, body, and soul. Sparking a bit of curiosity and leading you in a positive direction to eliminate any unnecessary forms of suffering or discomforts is my life's passion.

As you are taking in these words, filtering each letter through your eyes and processing them, you are storing the information in your subconscious mind. There, it will become an unbreakable habit branching off into every aspect of your existence. It will continue to grow and be utilized in each event, significant or insignificant, that comes into your vast experiences throughout your life. In truth, your interpretation of what is significant and insignificant may vary, but I am in high hopes that by the end of this book, you will possess the ability to find significance in the most insignificant situations. There is a lesson to be learned in everything, and in this, you will find the ultimate key to life!

Life may seem like a long journey while lingering and just existing in the present moment, but as the wise ones say, "A lifetime is just a heartbeat in heaven." Eternity awaits us all. So, my dear friends, shall we begin to learn the valuable lesson of appreciating every boring moment that is given?

The first thing I want you to do when you open those beautiful, enchanting eyes when you awake from a deep sleep is to give thanks and praise to the Creator—God—for the gift of a new day. Reach up to the heavens with your hands. Reach so far up into the sky that you feel a warm pressure throughout your shoulders, elbows, wrists, and fingers. While you are reaching into the heavens, I want you to imagine and feel the beautiful energy coming from God and his mighty angels. But most importantly, I want you to send your infinite love and gratitude to them. A beautiful exchange of love and gratitude will be taking place, a sacred dance. Imagine powerful waves of energy coming from your heart and sacral center out through your fingertips. Visualize your energy and what it is made of, including the color, the texture, and the fragrance of your essence. At the same time, imagine a beautiful light filled with an ethereal substance falling like crystalized snowflakes onto you from heaven.

Sing their praise! And feel their divine blessing!

Glory be to God in the highest!

Below is a prayer I would like to share with you. It always makes me feel awesome!

> Thank you, God, my divine Father, for this blessed day! Thank you, angels, for protecting me and guiding me toward health, peace, and abundance and fulfilling my soul's purpose in serving you through all that is pure, holy, and divine.
> Amen.

Remember it is right and just to give thanks, my dear friends! Giving thanks and praise to our heavenly Father is the most powerful form of gratitude. And the more habitual you are, the better you will feel. Your overall life experiences will become much more enhanced and elevated to the highest levels. This I can promise you without a single doubt in my mind. Your overall human experience will become magnificent and astonishingly magnified to the most elevated states of being. Pure bliss and joy will encompass you and all you say and do.

Once you start initiating this early-morning exercise every day, praising God and the divine, a holy energy of pure love will begin to brighten your life like a growing flame. You will soon glow and radiate with such a powerful, angelic light that it can only come from the true source itself: God. God longs for us to be beings of light and love, so we can live up to our fullest potential and fulfill the divine purpose for which we have been placed upon this earth. We all have a purpose here and now, at this very moment.

Being childlike and never losing your curiosity and enthusiasm throughout your life is vital. Keeping an innocent state of being during all the experiences that come into your life—negative or positive—will serve you in the purest ways. As children, we are constantly in a state of observance, like a sponge soaking it in. A child has an open mind that tends to be less judgmental and more accepting of people and events. We all have an inner child that craves nourishment. Remain in a beautiful, innocent state of being throughout your life, as much as possible. So singing, dancing, jumping up and down on the bed in the morning, and being the embodiment of joy and excitement is not immature. It's awesome, and it feels amazing! Every day you're alive and well is a soul celebration!

The purpose of integrating powerful routines into your daily life is to facilitate and usher in the divine providence and receive messages from angels and develop the ability to access the higher self, which is your spirit in the purest form.

I strongly urge you to focus on the divine and what your higher self brings forth during your time of prayer and/or meditations. It may be brought forth by—but not limited to—thoughts, feelings, sensations, emotions, words, sounds, colors, images, or even fragrance. Listen carefully to your inner voice and The Angels when you are seeking affirmations and guidance from God and the divine. All senses must be open and all the above must be kept in mind during prayer and meditation and while seeking communion with the divine.

Contemplate the information that came forward. Ask yourself these specific questions: "Did it bring me joy? Happiness? Excitement? Peace?" These are all important signs meant to reassure you that you're on the right path and being led by the holy divine.

If you feel uneasy or hesitant about any of the sensory

information that is being brought forth into your experience, these are signals that need to be considered. In that case, please proceed with caution. To proceed with caution means to think about it thoroughly. Pray or meditate on it longer and focus on the positive vibrations. Move away from the doubts, confusion, or discomforts.

When a specific feeling enters your experience, your body has key receptors known as instincts, intuition, inclination, or a sixth sense. This dwells within us all. It's important for us to heed its calling. We use it for protection (internal and external), and it is a primal factor that is inherent in us.

Developing our gifts of instincts and intuition over time is important and useful throughout our human life. Acknowledging that we have an instinct to begin with is a great way to start the process of development. When you get the sense to not eat a certain food or even go on a date with a certain someone, it's for a purpose.

Your higher self knows what's around that corner, and the result may not serve you. The development of your instincts will lead you to determine whether it's out of fear or out of an instinctual awareness. That's why it's crucial.

It is in the soul's and higher self's best interest to pray three times a day—morning, noon, and night— to maintain a constant connection with God, Mother Mary, Angels and The Saints. Always keep a constant line of communication open with the divine so you may be reached at any time. Having an open heart, mind, and spirit will bring you endless joy as well as peace of mind. You'll also have a sense of fulfillment, just by knowing you are connected and have established a pure connection. It's like a telepathic line that supersedes a telephone.

If you prefer to take a moment of peace, meditation, or silence, please do so at any time of day that is convenient for you. Pause and take a moment's breath, focusing on the blessings in your life. Also take time to place your intentions, goals, and what you wish to accomplish. Visualize it coming to fruition, imagine and feel the excitement as if you have already achieved it.

Placing your focus on the blessings in your life will enhance your awareness and guide you to your soul's purpose and life path. Sitting in silence, in an asana pose or Indian style, will help clear your mind and keep you focused. Clearing your space from negative energies, emotions, and vibrations is key. Lighting white candles and incense instantly enhances your positive vibrations. Using candlelight and fragrances unlocks the subconscious mind and enhances the current conscious state by utilizing the dominating senses and combining all the olfactory systems simultaneously. This plays a key role in transmitting positive signals to the brain and will be very relaxing for you—a sweet escape of sorts. I like to use palo santo and white sage to clear my space, especially in times of prayer.

Unlocking the voice of your higher self through meditation or prayer is the proper way of clearing one's mind. It provides an opportunity for the mind to declutter so you are truly able to focus. It is an opportunity to hear the divine energies and tune into the frequencies of God, The Angels, and the infinite universe, of which we are all sons and daughters. We are all made of stardust. It's a magical fact, not fiction! Remember that you are destined for greatness! The purest way to discover yourself and what God has placed you on the earth for is by self-reflection and total surrender of all fears and doubts to the Almighty and his angels. Fear and doubt are key emotions that hold us back from being the people we are destined to be. Whenever a tidal wave of fear and doubt comes into our minds and hearts, we are paralyzed and operating from the lowest vibration. Have faith that God, Queen of The Angels (Mother Mary), and The Angels are with you and have control over all things in your life. One of my favorite sayings I have ever come across was while I was browsing through greeting cards at the grocery store. Ironically enough, one stood out among the rest. It had a magical, white unicorn on the cover, and when I opened it, to my surprise, it had a recording of a sweet voice that said, "Miracles are everywhere!" Yes, indeed, they are, and they happen every second of every day! Praise be to God!

CHAPTER 2
POWER OF GRATITUDE

There is a divine bond between you and God when mastering the art of gratitude. Being grateful for all that takes place in your life is the greatest gift you can give God.

You may have heard the saying, "The attitude of gratitude," and there is so much happiness within this state of being. "Counting your blessings" is also a common phrase, and it's a perfect definition of gratitude. When we count our blessings, we are not only counting them, we are focusing on our gifts and appreciating how truly blessed we are. All those blessings will branch out, reaching for the sunlight like the blossoming flowers we are. Your countless blessings will not only show you how loved you are but also that you're truly provided for in every way.

Obtaining an attitude of gratitude is hard work! To achieve it truly, you need to make a religious habit out of it, day in and day out, moment to moment. It is the ability to express to your higher self and the divine providence that you are grateful and appreciate all the aspects of your life, both grand and minimal alike. From the shoes on your feet to the comfort of your bed and warm sheets, there is always time to relay to the heavens and God how grateful you are for being provided for.

When you are in a true state of gratitude, your energy will shift, and it will become a beautiful force that people around you will begin to feel. While you are in the divine state of gratitude, the power inside of you will begin to create and manifest the most beautiful experiences. Exercising the attitude of gratitude is the most reliable way to maximize your enjoyment while you are on the path to fulfilling your soul's purpose, bringing forth the divine energy to see it through and support you till the end.

Your overall mood will increase, thus increasing the serotonin levels in the brain, which are the main composites of joy and happiness. The increase in your positive mood will result in an increase in vibration. Your body will have nothing else to do but keep up with the mind and bring forth the overflowing joy that has been set in motion.

Is your cup half empty or half full? I want you, mentally, to be filled with such positivity and optimism that your cup will have to take on a new shape just to hold the amount of the finest, purest water. Blessings will multiply just because you are in a constant state of gratitude, and they will naturally flow into every part of your existence. Undeniable abundance, optimism, enthusiasm, and all other positive emotions will manifest through your physical attributes as well. This divine energy increase will result in positive deeds and actions toward your fellow man. Positive mind, positive body, positive action. Given this vital information, should there even be a single doubt in your mind to know that being in a constant state of gratitude will also alleviate any unnecessary suffering like, but not limited to, depression, anxiety, doubt, fear, and all other negative energies? It will ward off anything that does not serve you and your higher self. By being thankful, you will be filling the space so nothing negative will be able to penetrate the feeling of gratitude. You must occupy the space in your mind, body, and spirit with gratitude. Maximizing your gratitude equals happiness and abundance.

When we were children, one of the first things we did when we woke up in the morning was jump up and down on the bed! We were filled with such joy and had tremendous excitement for the day. Jumping up and down on the bed when you wake up in the morning sends a signal (frequency) to God and The Angels that you are happy, excited, and grateful for all you have been blessed with. The divine will continue to bestow blessings upon your life in more ways than you can count. This is because you are truly happy and content with what you have been given, and thus your spirit is open to receiving more abundance in different forms like, but not limited to, wisdom, faith, hope, purity, virtue, health, abundance, fruitful relationships, a fulfilling career, ideas, opportunities to serve the holy, divine, mother earth, and all those who inhabit it, including adults, children, plants, animals, and all other life forms. The gifts that are given to us by our holy Father in heaven and The Angels who carry out God's will to serve, protect, and provide us with endless blessings deserve our praise and recognition. This reminds me of a story I once heard and would like to share with you.

There was a boy who was unable to walk. Staring out his window at a man who was running on the street below, the little boy said to himself, "Oh God, if I could only walk, I'd run and play all day!"

The man he saw running at that very moment was

staring at a man riding a bicycle, and he said to himself, "If I only had the money to buy a bike, I'd get to where I need to go much faster!"

The man riding the bike was staring at a man driving a car and thought to himself, you guessed it! *If I could only afford to buy a car.* The moral of the story is, always appreciate what you have because there is someone in the world who wishes with all their heart they had the ability to see the above taking place.

Being in a state of gratitude will be a great relief for you during moments when you are experiencing discomfort or being subjected to forms of negative energies, which happens to us all, unfortunately. We are human and do falter to our negative thoughts, but this will be a test for you and your ability to power flip. It means to flip the negative thought into a positive one, since you are more capable of controlling your thoughts and harness that ability within you. We all have that divine power within us.

Make it a daily routine to focus on all the beauty in your life and all the beauty that surrounds you. In return, the negative thought will only be for a moment, and it will have no other choice but to vacate the mind, body, and spirit. As soon as you flip your focus onto the positive, which are your gifts from God, you will begin to feel the positive vibrations in and around you. Start by counting your blessings, and you will see the miracles in your life, which are truly never-ending. Continue to practice this, and the rest will fall into place like a beautiful puzzle. Piece by piece, it will effortlessly connect your mind, body, and soul back into harmony and remove all chaos. When we experience negative energy, it is a small form of chaos, and we are no longer in harmony. So, remember to exercise your power and control by flipping your negative thoughts into positive ones.

> Manifesting greatness by being grateful
> is the greatest practice, leading to even
> greater achievements.
> —Roxanne Saint Marie.

Those who come into your life will feel your positive, magnetic energy. It is like a force field gravitating to you, like the earth orbiting the sun. Those who are attracted to light will be drawn to you. Those who enter your life will help bring change and awareness into your experience and assist you in your journey to fulfill your life's purpose in the most exciting and profound ways!

Others who do not serve your higher self, meaning your best interest, will fall to the wayside. When you start to operate from a higher frequency, some of your closest friends and even family members will not be welcomed into your experience anymore. You may have noticed negative situations or events occur while you're in the presence of these friends and family members. There will be telling signs. For example, we all have that one friend who loves to drink and party—who thrives off being the center of attention. They can be a lot of fun. However, what goes up must come down. Cue the pendulum swing! That attention seeker will likely attract the wrong person, potentially putting you in a dangerous situation or in harm's way. When you're with your so-called friends and they are judgmental of your life choices, gossip about others, and make comments about your clothes, your makeup, or other superficial aspects of your appearance, think twice. These people are not a positive influence in your life. They are quite the opposite, in fact. When you're in their low vibrational field, like a wave, it will come crashing down on you. You will feel the effects of their negative energy and vibrations. While in their presence, you'll have feelings of worry, uneasiness, nervousness, and anxieties. You will suddenly begin to doubt yourself, doubting the way you're dressed, wondering if you look beautiful or if your makeup is on perfectly. You might ask yourself, "I wonder if they talk about me behind my back." This is your higher self, and your body reacting in a fight-or-flight response, which is a primal drive. Those who are not on the same spiritual level or operate from their heart and soul will kindly be escorted out of your life, making way for those who are there to lift you up and place your best interest first, making room for those who are there to encourage you to be the best version of yourself. You will feel safe and comfortable around them and get feelings of ease, comfort, acceptance, and unconditional love. Those are the types of relationships that truly add value to our lives and bring peace to the depths of our soul.

Speaking in truth, the only reason people bring others down is to lower their vibration by matching it to their own. Have you ever heard the phrase "cut you down to size"? They feel negatively themselves, thus projecting that negativity onto you. It may also be that they have been treated that way in the past, resulting in a referential experience. Remember this old saying: "Misery loves company." There are so many truths in this saying, and it is brought into our experience for a purpose (a warning). These types of individuals are brought into our experience for a reason. It is solely to help us understand how we should treat others. Another beautiful saying is, "Do unto others as you would have them do unto you."

Remember this golden rule in life: "What you put out is what you get back, threefold."

If you are in a toxic relationship, it is meant to teach you about yourself, your desires, your self-control, what you can and cannot handle. What you truly desire out of a relationship. Once you have gone through the birth pains and lessons of the relationship with strength and courage, you will be rewarded. If you do not have the strength to walk away or end it, the heavens will make the way for you. They will bring forth a negative experience hoping that you will wake up and say, "Enough is enough. I'm done with this! The lesson has been taught and paid in full."

Out with the old and in with the new!

When you truly possess an attitude of gratitude, you will begin to attract positive, fulfilling experiences in your life. You will desire more beauty, opportunity, peace, love, and abundance in your daily life. Speaking through your heart, coming from a place of true love and gratitude, is the absolute best for you and all those who surround you. Gratitude is divine medicine. No matter how you are currently feeling in your life, your job isn't going as well as you expected, you are suffering from illness, or you broke up with the love of your life. Remember and rest assured that it will get better! You will heal! You will love again! This too shall pass, as does everything in life, moment by moment. As the sun rises and sets again and again, the universe is constantly expanding, and so are you. The universe inside of you and all around you is continuously changing and rearranging to better serve you, and your higher self is aware of it all. Remember, everything happens for a reason, and everything is in divine order.

Stop and smell the roses throughout your life, and I do mean this literally. Throw the petals above your head and watch the beautiful light shine through them as they fall upon you, blessing you with their sweet smell and ethereal essence. Take these moments and dive into the endless amounts of beauty and soak it in.

Let it resonate and be sure to store it in your memory.

Look around you! Seek beauty and you will find beauty in all things. This is also a divine act of gratitude.

All of God's creation is made of light, energy, vibrations, and frequencies, as well as the most beautiful ethereal substances. Sacred geometry is in everything from a rock to a rose. It's truly amazing to see, and our Creator is even more amazing. How did he do it? We are too small to understand but do reap the benefits of God's gifts daily and must always see things with eyes of gratitude. No matter what happens in our lives, we will go on, as the glorious sun will rise again, as birds will wake, chirping and rejoicing at sunrise. They sing their praises to the Almighty. Birds are angelic creatures and bring us humans so much joy and sweet music if we choose to listen. We can learn so much from our tiny winged friends, and what I find most fascinating about them is that they are everywhere, with us and watching over us. They add value to our experience by the enchanting frequencies they adorn us with, as well as their good luck droppings. They are little angels in some form or another. From the busy streets of Los Angeles to the deserted deserts of Arabia, they will always make their angelic voices heard for all who care to listen.

Morning, noon, or night, or any time in between, it is important for us to reconnect with our Creator (God), to pause for a moment and think of the many blessings we have in our lives and the gift of the present moment, here and now.

I'd like to share something with you that not too many people know about me. I enjoy writing daily prayers to God, Jesus, Mother Mary, and The Angels. I write daily prayers and affirmations on paper. I feel that this is an important aspect of practicing gratitude, and if it were adopted by everyone, it will continue to create abundance in all our lives and bring us closer to God in return. You will build a closer relationship with heaven, and that is more valuable than all the gold in the world.

Keep a beautiful notebook just for you and God. If you do not believe in God or Jesus, that's okay! I am not here to judge. I'm simply here to share my truth and my experiences. We human beings have different types of beliefs, and that difference is what makes us human, beautiful in our own ways.

Slowly but surely, what you write on paper will become your reality.

Here's an example of one of my letters to God.

Thank you, Father God in heaven, for this blessed day. I give thanks and praise to you, The Angels and The Saints above watching over me, every moment of every day. May you continue to bless my life with health, love, abundance, and peace. Thank you for all the blessings you have bestowed upon my life. I pray your will be done above all else, and may your love and light continue to shine upon me so I may shine upon others with the light and love that you have blessed me with. I pray to do your will alone throughout my life, and may you bless my life with a divine purpose to serve others and the divine accordance through the grace and wisdom that is you. I give thanks for your protection against all negative energies that do not serve me but wish me harm. In Jesus's holy name. Amen.

CHAPTER 3
POWER OF DREAMS

Dreams are the key to unlocking the

doors of our subconscious mind.

To dream is a miracle in and of itself. When we lay our heads down to rest and close our eyes, we shut off the conscious mind and journey into the unknown. That is our subconscious—traveling through doors and entering places that we never knew existed. We experience images, sensations, smells, and experiences that have never entered our thoughts or ever crossed our minds while awake.

I heard a saying once that has remained with me over the years: "God shows us his power in our dreams and reveals his will in our visions." There are several verses in the Holy Bible that refer to dreams. The one below is by far my favorite.

And he said, Hear my words; If there is a prophet among you, I the Lord make myself known to him in a vision; I speak with him in a dream. (Numbers 12:6)

In the Bible, there is a story about a man (Joseph) who was chosen by God, and God revealed his mighty plans to him through visions and dreams. The visions and dreams that where bestowed upon Joseph were meant for the king of Egypt so that he would heed God's warning. Joseph interpreted dreams for the king as well, and through that, he gained the trust of the Egyptian king, served and lived alongside him, and was given the sacred task to oversee the land of Egypt. His visions and dreams saved the people from famine, which was the ultimate destruction and symbol of doom in that time.

So how do we know for sure where dreams come from or what they are made of? Some philosophers will argue the fact that dreaming is a hallucination, while others say it's our imagination gone wild from gathered thoughts and stored information that have been acquired throughout our lives.

After all the years of research and studies on dreams and visions, we still do not have a definite, scientific answer as to why we dream. Amazing, right? With all the technical advances humans have made throughout the centuries, some things are meant to remain in the realm of miracles.

Maybe dreams are windows into other dimensions, alternate realities, or as the ancient Egyptians believed, a looking glass into our future or the future of others. Most ancient cultures have a very beautiful way of interpreting dreams. The Egyptians created "The Book of Dreams," dated to the early reign of Ramesses II (1279–1213 BC).

The ancient Greeks also had a book on dream interpretation that was created by Artemidorus in the second century AD. He left behind a book that focused on the interpretations of animals, people, symbols, and their meanings in relation to dreams.

Throughout history, there have been many cases of people having dreams and visions of angels guiding and instructing them to carry out God's will on earth.

Saint Michael appeared to Joan of Arc when she was just thirteen years old. In her vision, Saint Michael told her that she would be visited by Saint Catharine and Saint Margret and to follow their counsel and guidance. Her visions of The Saints gave her purpose, and she found the power through the divine to carry out a task that would seem impossible for a man, yet alone a thirteen-year-old girl. She took up arms, led the army of France against the English, and was victorious. She will be remembered for all time, and her visions are what made her a legend and a Saint.

Many prophets have had prophetic dreams and visions

that foretold the future. Nostradamus, for example, worked and advised the most powerful queen of France in that time, Kathrine De' Medici. Nostradamus is known for his Quatrains. His visions were predictions that foretold the distant future and are still coming into fruition till this day!

Almost every king or queen throughout history has had a man or prophet in their closest circle to interpret their dreams and give insight about the future of their Kingdom and their very lives.

Many people seek out those who can interpret dreams or foretell their future. It's in our nature to want to know our future. Always remember to trust God and place your life in his hands and become a divine instrument. We have the ability to pray and seek counsel from God and The Angels about our dreams. Turn to God.

Powerful information is revealed in dreams and visions, and it's a blessing.

I have had the most beautiful, vivid dreams where I am able to smell, taste, and touch. I once dreamt I was swimming in a cool, crystal blue pool of water, playing with angelic seahorses that were as colorful as the rainbow, yet translucent. I was collecting starfish and seashells underwater without even having to come up for a breath of air. There are so many magical, enchanting experiences that we can obtain and manifest in the dream world that we cannot wrap our heads around. I am always left with unanswered questions: How did I get access to this magical place? When can I go back? How did I imagine this in the first place?

The poles of polarity are ever so present, and I can assure you that my nightmares of sea monsters sure make me appreciate those angelic seahorses!

If you awaken from a nightmare and it has upset your morning, still give thanks, pray, and ask for guidance and interpretation from the divine providence. Consider researching the meaning online. This will alleviate some discomforts because God and The Angels will speak to us through all our dreams, both good or bad. It is all through interpretation.

Remember that to awake from sleep is a miracle in and of itself. Our bodies possess the power and ability to wake and even know how to breathe during it all. Amazing, right? To be able to travel in our dreams, taste, smell, and touch. The fact that our senses are not laid to rest is sublime! Our minds are literally awake and conjuring up the most beautiful images and at times the most frightening.

I've had nightmares where I woke up crying out of my sleep, begging my long-lost love not to leave me. I've had nightmares of an anaconda sleeping at my feet and I was paralyzed with fear. Both, I must admit, were quite frightening and on two entirely different levels—one emotional and one physical.

There have been times when I awoke from a dream in such pain, fear, and sorrow that it brought forth suffering. The very memory of it would trigger my emotions. I remember once when I woke up, I said, "This is going to be a very hard day." I would replay the dream (event) in my mind all day long, trying to find the meaning. I would ask myself, *Why did I dream that? How?* in an endless attempt to shake the discomfort. Unfolding events throughout the day only amplified the negative emotions and brought forth negative representations in correlation to it all. The only way I can truly describe it is like being caught in a paradigm in your mind. There is nowhere to go but spinning out of control and on repeat. This stems from a lack of understanding and wisdom that my words led me to subconsciously attract negative experiences throughout the day, from the barista at the coffee shop getting my order wrong, to misplacing important items, to getting cut off by a truck and almost crashing. They all add small forms of chaos throughout my day. When these events occur simultaneously, any sane person would say, "Hey! That's out of your control!" But I'm here to tell you, we are more in control than we've been led to believe. When I woke up, what did I say out loud? Do you remember? I said, "This is going to be a very hard day," and just like magic, it became what I said it would. More so, I believed it, which made it even more powerful! I was totally unaware that I was cursing myself and my day.

Words are like magic, a double-edged sword. They can create peace, chaos, blessings or curses, love, and hate. My day felt like everything was going wrong, and it was. I felt utterly trapped in my own chaotic reality, and finally, I had enough! I fell to my knees when I found a moment to be alone, and I prayed. After feeling the strength given from above, I began the process of talking to myself, assuring myself that everything was okay, and I removed all that did not serve me, my higher self, and my soul. I began to research my dream and its meaning, seeking counsel from God and heaven above, asking out loud for help and guidance. It brought peace back into my world, relieving all forms of stress and anxieties. I was slowly but surely regaining my strength by consistently fighting off the thought (memory) of my dream that was the bane of my day.

Ultimately dreams become a part of our experience. Dreams have the power to create memories. Have you ever thought to yourself, *I can't remember if that was a dream or reality* when presented with a memory that enters your mind days or even months after the dream originally occurred? It's happened to me, several times, in fact. However, if you're a person who doesn't dream at all or can't remember them, then deem yourself very special, and you must be able to conjure up some major daydreams!

CHAPTER 4
POWER OF THOUGHT AND WORD

Wisdom comes from the depths

of our being that is the infinite

universe and the Creator thereof.

Gaining the wisdom and sacred knowledge to erase and release all conflicting thoughts that are not serving our higher selves is a divine lesson in and of itself. Some say we are reborn onto earth to continue our spiritual development. We are spiritual beings, and maybe we are longing to complete this level of sacred training, so we can move onto the next.

People say, "I can't control what my mind conjures up!" and this may have some truth to it, but what if I told you that it is possible to navigate your thoughts and maneuver them into the righteous path that is worthy of you?

Capture and harness the power within your mind to change your unworthy thoughts as soon as they appear.

It will transmute your emotions, your actions, and in due course, your realities. Who really enjoys having undesirable thoughts that bring about discomfort and unnecessary suffering anyway?

We can stop our minds from wandering into negative thought patterns, like reliving unpleasant memories or preconceived events that most likely will never happen. We can create future memories, so think of your greatest outcome, the best scenario that will bring you joy, happiness, excitement, and peace.

Imagine rewiring our minds so perfectly that they automatically turn a negative thought into a positive one. That's mastery! This is one of the hardest goals we will set to accomplish in our lives, but we are resilient creatures made of pure light, energy, and stardust. We are capable of so much greatness and don't give ourselves enough credit when it is due. And it is due right here, right now!

Know that mastering the above is vital for us as human beings in finding our true purpose. It will enrich and add value to our everyday lives and the lives of those we encounter. Being pure of thought, mind, and spirit will attract true divinity and will aid us in finding our soul's purpose and chosen path. Never forget to correct by redirecting your thought process and perception upon all situations that come into your experience.

The process of removing fears and anxieties are like the removal of negative thoughts but has a different process.

To remove these discomforts, we need to pinpoint the source of negative energy in our bodies. For example, people often describe it as, "It feels like a frog in my throat." That frog is more than what we consciously think it is, but the unconscious mind knows that it is a negative force that needs to be removed some way, somehow.

I am going to teach you a magic trick sent from heaven above. Are you ready? Here it comes ...

Close your eyes softly. Take a peaceful moment in a quiet place and center yourself, either by sitting in an asana pose or lying down on the floor. Do whatever feels best for you personally, since we are all uniquely different in our own special ways.

The main objective is to center and ground yourself mentally and physically.

Now, I want you to breathe in through your nose and out through your mouth. Listen to your life-giving breath and really tune into it. Take as much time as you need until you reach that peaceful moment where you are filled with calmness. Fill your space with harmonious energy. Feel it inside your body and all around you. Envelop yourself, and allow it to move through you. Once this is accomplished, it means you have cleared all negative vibrations. You are shifting the energy grid within and around you. Remember that everyone is different. Some people may need to take four deep breaths while others may need to take forty-four. When you have completed purifying your space, you will begin to feel like a weight has been lifted off your shoulders and may experience weightlessness. If you feel a sudden wave of chills come over your body, this means you have released all the negative energy and have been touched by the divine. Good work!

Now, once you have reached the magical realm of self-awareness and peaceful bliss, I want you to zone in and locate that specific area, like that suffocating frog in the throat. It can be other locations in your body where you may have experienced discomforts in the past. Focus on that specific spot, and start to imagine a bright light penetrating it, purifying that area. You can pierce it with an imaginary ethereal sword that belongs to Archangel Michael. Now as you see his ethereal blade made of golden light enter you, imagine all negative energy draining out the from entrance area of the blade of ethereal light. It could be a form of black fluid that comes pouring out, or it could be tiny nails. It solely depends on the person and their perception of the feeling or emotion.

There is no right or wrong here. Keep that in mind.

Envision the color pouring out from the source. There's a color in every energy form. When people say, "She was red with anger," or "green with envy," there is truth behind it—scientific proof, in fact!

Once you begin to feel that negative energy disappearing and dispensing from what I like to call the frog spot, imagine bluish-pink crystals or purple ether filling up that empty space. At the same moment, I want you to think of a beautiful memory that gave you joy and happiness. Place that beautiful memory image inside of your frog spot, and inside yourself. Fill yourself up with all the joy and happiness that moment brought you. It could also be a serene location, like a creek, twinkling stars, or playing with your favorite pet. You may also envision and insert words like love, peace, health, and healing. Again, it is different for everyone, and there are no specific rules. We all have our own unique memories that infinitely span across the universe, available in the Akashic hall of records—our "book of life." We truly are blessed to have access to those blissful memories, and they could bring us utter joy.

We have them stored in our minds for a purpose, and I believe it is to bring us joy in our present moments.

We have infinite access to our life files, including positive past events and experiences, as well as negative experiences. The poles of polarity are present in everything, but who wants to relive those negative memories anyways?

The above is a guideline to show you how positive

memories and emotions can be brought into our current experience and can be utilized to establish healing and relief from a negative situation.

> For the word of God is living and active, sharper than any two-edged sword, piercing to the division of souls and of spirit, of joints and of marrow, and discerning the thoughts and intentions of the heart. (Hebrews 4:12)

There is so much power behind the word. You can create harmony, or you can destroy. Every word that is spoken begins with a thought.

It is said in many cultures around the world that the universe and all things in it were created by the word.

In the Bible, it is said that God used the "word" to create the universe and all things in it.

In the Mahabharata, it is said that the spoken word, "Om," created the universe and all that is in it.

Broken down, what does the word consist of? It is sound frequencies, and those frequencies are vibrations that carry energy and capture the intentions within it. Words are powerful vibrations. They have a purpose to generate and create our reality.

There was a wonderful Japanese researcher, photographer, and entrepreneur named Dr. Masaru Emote, God bless his soul. He was specifically known for his water research and made his findings public.

Dr. Emote tested music, spoken words, and written words on the outside of glass jars that contained water. He acquired samples of the frozen water after being exposed to positive music and positive words. The water formed the most beautiful crystals in different shapes and sizes, mirroring the vibrations of the word or music (frequencies).

The phrases (words), "I love you," and "I hate you," were written on the outside of various glass jars that contained water and rice, and for thirty days, the formations that grew within each of the glass jars were *undeniable.* The glass jars with the written words, "I love you" upon them grew to be beautiful and consumable for the human body. The glass jars with the words, "I hate you" had grown to rot, and their contents were not consumable.

Starting now, when you drink a glass of water or eat, pray words of gratitude, health, peace, love, and abundance into it or over it.

The human body is made up of 60 percent water.

The heart and brain alone are made up of 73 percent water.

This knowledge is the finest and purest form of power.

There is an agreement I want you to make here and now, and it is to be impeccable and positive with your words. If you fall short, just remind yourself and take back what you said that was negative and replace it with something positive—a loving or kind thought—and then speak it aloud in your sweetest verbal tone three times. There is power in repetition and even more so if it is done in threes. I love you, I love you, I love you … Can you feel it?

Using sounds to heal rather than destroy, this power lies within us all. It's science, down to the molecular and quantum level. Each cell in your body reacts to all forms of energy.

This is a proven fact time and time again throughout scientific research.

Different sounds have different frequencies as well as colors. Tones being raised to the highest level will turn into octaves. Eventually, you will obtain the frequencies of light. Find a standard color chart, and apply it to the musical scale. You'll be amazed! The more you research about vibrations and their colors, the more you will begin to travel down the rabbit hole of knowledge. Follow the white rabbit!

Our ancient ancestors have been using sounds (vibrations) for various forms of healing and therapy. Take music, for example. We are beginning to use ancient methods of music for healing and to treat stress-related issues. Certain types of music are known to relieve stress and implement positive vibrations, creating a harmonious atmosphere for your cells to heal and thrive. Sickness in the body is a form of chaos within our cells. Every cell in our body is attracted to harmony and consciously moves away from organisms that cause disharmony. Everything in nature thrives in a harmonious environment like a flock of birds traveling to their sacred mating grounds in distant lands, or a school of fish traveling in the vast ocean.

There is an invisible realm …

What I find to be the most interesting about the invisible light and sound spectrum is although you cannot see it, it shouldn't imply that it does not exist, just like the spirit and soul.

Chapter 5
Power of Kindness

There is a divine power within those
who seek to extend their love and
kindness onto others. Love and
kindness are free and the greatest
gift a human being can give.

Acts of kindness are very important to the divine providence and to those who are at the receiving end of such kindness. The joy you will gain from seeing others happy from your good deeds will add value to your life and enrich your human experience, so much, in fact, that a ripple effect will create a beautiful wave into your heart and soul and will move aside any suffering you may have.

"No act of kindness, no matter how small, is ever wasted."

This classic old saying has so much wisdom laid within it, layer upon layer, like a sweet pomegranate fruit. Seed by seed, it is waiting to be peeled and consumed, ever so patiently for your physical and spiritual nourishment.

You will follow these words of wisdom because you value your life and your experiences. You value the human connection since it adds inner strengths and builds character, revealing so much about yourself. Throughout your life, various interactions with people in the end will bring you closer to becoming the best version of yourself.

Witness your true self as these revealing moments go on throughout your life, negative and positive alike. Thoughts and deeds will become ever more apparent. Reflect upon them and change what does not serve you and those you love. Find the power to change what you see fit and what does not bring you joy and peace. Stop and witness yourself at that very moment. Analyze your perception of others, situations, places, and things.

Ask yourself if your perception is negative or positive. Ask yourself if your judgment of that homeless person crossing the street is just. Is the anger you feel from suddenly being cut off while driving serving you in any way? I have felt the fire of anger from being cut off while driving since my hometown is Los Angeles, and it's well known for its traffic. Nevertheless, I can assure you, it does not in any way, shape, or form serve you, and your higher self knows this to be true. I am guilty of both and the battle is yet to be won, but if I try my hardest to stop and recognize these thoughts, emotions, and deeds as soon as they occur and turn my negative energy around, I am creating positive change. Recognizing and implementing positive change will create a ripple effect, reaching out into the world. My anger is only going to attract negative energy upon myself and others. Trace it and locate the general association with discomforts, since that's where it stems from.

A negative feeling or thought comes from an association with a person, place, or thing. It's stored in our memories, whether it was installed into our subconscious mind through society or by influence from those closest to us during our childhood, which, in truth, shapes us to be who we are as adults. Even if you don't consciously realize it, 95 percent of the time it can be traced back to our childhood. How did your mother and father respond to someone who cut them off when driving while you were in the backseat? How did they treat a homeless person who approached them? It's a primal drive indeed for a parent to protect their child. However, most of the time that homeless person or driver was innocent in their actions and had no ill intent. As children, we soaked up everything we heard like a sponge. We adopted behaviors from those who surrounded us and those we admired.

As adults, we are susceptible to the ideals and beliefs of those who are brought into our current experience without our permission through mainstream media, like actors, musicians, athletes, presidents, and queens.

Each one of us has a unique, soulful purpose, not

only regarding human beings but all life forms on earth, from the smallest bees set on a path to pollinate fruit trees to feed our hungry bellies to a homeless man placed in our path at the right place and time to teach us compassion and humility. I personally think in some cases they are angels sent to earth to teach us and witness us—to witness our behaviors and the way we interact with people (angels in disguise). Certain situations reveal to God who we truly are. That reminds me of a story I'd like to share. This story is a personal experience that has impacted my life, and I will remember it forever.

One day I was with a friend, parking our cars on a busy street after a long day at the beach, and a little girl approached us and looked up at my friend with her big brown eyes and said with the sweetest voice, "Excuse me, miss, do you have two dollars?"

She must have been seven or eight years old and completely alone, pushing a little cart with a dolly in it.

She literally came out of thin air. There were no adults around as far as the eye could see.

My friend responded, "No, I'm sorry, sweetie. I don't have any money."

The little girl looked up at us both, smiled, and said, "Okay, thank you!"

I was endlessly searching through my bag the moment she asked even though I knew I had no money, hoping to find something to give her, and as soon as she turned around and began to walk away, I found a five-dollar bill and was so excited! I had no idea where this five-dollar bill came from in all honesty. I truly don't remember having it, because earlier that day I wanted to leave a cash tip for the waitress at lunch and I had no cash, so I put it on my credit card instead.

I called out, ran toward her, and said, "Wait! Here! I found this!" and handed it to her.

She replied, "Oh thank you so much and God bless you. You are an angel."

I asked her, "How come?"

Her response was, "Because I only asked for two dollars and you gave me five, and I know that this is all you have left to spend. God bless you."

I said, "I wish I had more to give and thank you. God bless you, little angel. Is everything okay? Do you live close by?"

She said yes, smiled, and walked away. We watched her turn the corner and disappear.

Do you believe in angels? Well, they believe in you, and they come in all shapes and sizes. So, keep your heart open to the possibilities of a blessed encounter, and God will surely amaze you. He loves to contact us in the most precious ways.

When you see an opportunity to serve someone, take it, like an elderly man or woman crossing the street.

Take their hand and guide them. Compliment her dress or his hat and talk about the weather. These are truly special occasions and are sacred moments captured in space and time. You will be doing good works, showing love and tenderness to those who want to be loved and valued, as well as remembered. In my heart of hearts, I feel that God is watching us always (even if it is through the eyes of birds perched above us). And all we do is being recorded in the Akashic records (The Book of Life). Sometimes I feel that when we are presented with an opportunity to serve, it could be an angel sent from heaven to interact with us, and that is our true time to shine like the light workers we aspire to be.

Keep your head up, and lock eyes with people on the street or when you're out and about in the world. Take the time to look around you. Surround yourself with love and light, and smile at people. Say hello. It will empower you in many ways and will build up your confidence levels and increase the serotonin in your brain, which will bring you joy. Be advised, not everyone is going to smile back, and that may sting your ego, but that ego needs fine tuning. What better way to tone it down then being "rejected" or in truth a perceived rejection. This is a mild form of rejection and good practice for you. Remember to observe your reactions upon the initial perceived rejection and never take it personally, since you have no idea what is going on in that person's life. It ultimately has nothing to do with you and everything to do with their current experience.

It's difficult to find the exact number of how many people we will encounter throughout our lives. Some say it will be somewhere between ten thousand and twenty thousand for the average person, which, of course, solely depends on the person and whether he or she has an active social life, or due to his or her career, interacts with many people daily.

Chapter 6
Power of Energy

All of God's creation has a
frequency, an energy, a divine spark
of intelligence that supersedes
all human understanding.

You must come to realize here and now, at this very moment, that you possess the ability to create powerful energies (negative and positive) that can shape and shift the energy in a room as well as the energy within those you share your life (experience) with.

The energy that exudes from a human being can be so contagious that you automatically (unconsciously) match their frequency. For example, there is a video of a man on a train in NYC who starts to watch a video on his cellphone and begins laughing uncontrollably. On the visible spectrum, you can see his face and other extremities of his body speak the language of pure joy, but what lies within the invisible spectrum? What's accruing that does not meet the eye? There is a high magnitude of energy and vibration that he is emitting. His vibration is spreading throughout the train like wildfire, with such force that everyone has no choice but to start laughing hysterically.

Scientists call this mirror neuron system or MNS for short. I believe it's human energy transfer, plain and simple.

The true explanation of mirror neurons is a special group of neurons that mirror implicated neurocognitive functions like social cognition, language, empathy, theory of mind, and neuropsychiatric disorders. Basically, the recognition of others' motor actions and emotions that are all within your proximity—that is your energy field.

The sooner you realize the invisible field of quantum energy is fact and not fiction, you will begin to have the ability to recognize the energy while it is occurring. Once this realization occurs, you will have the ability to change energy frequencies by admitting light, positive energy, and love, manipulating the neurons that surround us and our energy field on a quantum, metaphysical level. If we utilize that energy, we can create a grid to protect ourselves and those we love from all negative outside influences and frequencies.

The more you practice this sacred knowledge of awareness, the more powerful you will become in your efforts.

Now your ideas for your life's purpose may be irrational to others and deemed unattainable by their belief system. Whether your dream and life's purpose is to be living on a ranch in the middle of nowhere, herding sheep, growing vegetables, and living a self-sustaining life, or becoming a movie star with the means to inspire by your inspirational story of rags to riches or maybe dedicate your life to charity work, stay true to it. Your dreams, visions, ideas, and goals maybe so farfetched to those in your closest circle, like your coworkers, friends, and family. Their mentality is filled with lack of belief and understanding, and you will ultimately adopt this reality if you're not careful and have the wisdom to see the signs while it is occurring. You can get caught in a whirlpool of unnecessary suffering caused by self-doubt.

Remember, when two states of existence share the same space, the higher state of existence will naturally override the weaker state. This is also a scientific fact. It is called octave resonance—a transfer of energy. A good example is the vibrations that manifest between two people. Given the circumstance, it could be quite a powerful game of tennis or a ping-pong match. Two energies are bouncing back and forth, until finally they either synchronize, meaning one dominates the other, or until harmony is found and an agreement is formed. The reason you feel the power of love or hate exuding from someone is due to the powerful frequency behind it.

Every frequency has an associated color. Love feels

like love, and hate feels like hate. Both are extremely powerful, so keep that in mind while you're involved in an energy exchange, be well trained, and have your racket ready. Be bold, courageous, and strong in your beliefs, and by the power of your conviction, you will become an unbreakable, unshakable force to be reckoned with. It is not about your advantage or ability to one-up the other person; it comes from inside of you, the core of your belief system. You truly don't owe anyone an explanation, but I do encourage you to express yourself, and by that alone, your powerful vibrations will far exceed those who challenge you and your purpose.

It is in your best interest to be aware that people possess the power to talk you out of achieving your soul's purpose by their ideals, logic, and so-called reason.

Others literally can shift your pattern of thinking by mere suggestion. They are not thinking of your best interest. They are merely seeking to validate themselves and their beliefs. This is a primal drive and an act of power and control. What better way to validate that person than to completely abandon your set course and belief system that may lead you to self-discovery and ultimately finding and fulfilling your life purpose. People, in general, want to reinforce their ideals and beliefs by impacting other lives, by using either negative or positive reinforcements. Maintain your focus on those who seek to motivate you through positive actions, for example, words of affirmation, acts of encouragement, and support of any kind. Those are positive people, and their words and actions are worthy of remaining in your conscious, unconscious, and subconscious mind.

Remember, those who are negative are ultimately seeking affirmations to validate their own feelings and doubts that are based solely off fear. Look at their lives, their accomplishments, and the way they operate and interact with people. Consider their overall outlook on past or current situations in their life experience. Also, look at their outlook on people, the world, places, and things. You can tell a lot by a person who is undeniably negative, and it will reflect in all areas of their existence.

Be powerful and bold when believing in yourself and your life choices. However "good" their intentions may be or how well they verbally express themselves and come across, it is still their truth and their perceived perception of you and your dreams, whatever that may be. Their perceived perception, however, does have the ability and power to alter your inner and outer universe.

Fear not! This is only if you allow it!

You must not be susceptible to their fears and doubts, their underlining sabotages or negative perceptions. Sacrificing your beliefs and taking on the belief of another is a form of self-sabotage in and of itself. If your plan is to achieve in finding your higher self and your soul's purpose, you must have the power of your conviction.

Every soul has a purpose and a calling. It is different for everyone. Just as everyone possesses different DNA and fingerprints, we are all bound to have a different purpose, and it's no one's place to infringe upon that, ever!

It is so amazing how different each human being on this earth is. We are all beautiful, unique, cosmic miracles on a fast track to spiritual development through achieving our soul purpose. In a perfect world, everyone would embrace each other's differences and support each other's efforts to fulfill their dreams and soul purpose. What a beautiful world that would be!

Remember, human beings are driven and motivated throughout their life by purpose alone, and without this, we become empty, hollow shells of ourselves, wandering throughout the world and attempting to navigate the treacherous terrain with a cloak over our eyes. We must lift the veil of tears and see the true world and witness its mysteries.

Nothing will impede you while you're on a personal journey to finding yourself and fulfilling your soul purpose.

It's important to remember that people who do not serve your higher self or add value to your spiritual growth are not worthy of your time and energy. However, during the process of that relationship, you are gaining wisdom and acquiring needed knowledge for spiritual progression, and it has been brought into your experience for a reason. These unfulfilling situations allow us to grow as individuals. The lessons learned from a failed relationship, in truth, are not a failure. You learn so much from a relationship—what's most valuable to you and what is not. In translation, you learn what serves your higher self and brings you joy and what does not. You grow from this, and certain unpleasant situations, like an argument, can lead to the power of finding your truths and beliefs. Many souls (people) will come into your experience throughout your life's journey. People are meant to teach us key lessons about ourselves. For example, these include but not limited to patience, forgiveness, compassion, and the overall achievement of controlling one's emotions.

This extends to the way we interact with all life forms on this big blue planet we call home. Again, every organism on this planet has a consciousness, from the birds to the bees, the pollen, and the trees. Everything that comes into your experience is meant to teach your soul a valuable lesson. When a mouse enters our house, the first thing we want to do is be rid of it, hence the invention of a mouse trap, and arguably so. Mice and rats are believed to carry infectious diseases like the black plague that almost wiped out all of Europe in the 1300s.

However, let's flip the poles of polarity, shall we?

There is a sacred place in India that thousands of rats call home, and it's known as Karni Mate Temple, a.k.a. "The Temple of Rats." These holy rats are called *kabbas*, and many people come from near and far to pay their respects. Many people drink the water and eat the same food as these "holy rats" at the temple. The people say, "It's a great honor to share food and water with these rats." Ironically enough, there has never been an outbreak of disease or an epidemic recorded at the temple or surrounding area since its existence.

When I was five years old, I found a mouse stuck in a hole. It's little butt was sticking out, and it was kicking its back legs in a panic, determined to get through.

I screamed out loud, "Mom! there's a mouse in the house!"

Our initial reaction was based off fear, or at least

mine was. The first thing we did was grab a knife from the kitchen, and we were prepared to kill it.

I asked her, "What are we going to do? Chop it in half?"

She stopped, put the knife down, and said, "No, it's innocent. We went back into the kitchen, grabbed a dish glove, and pushed its little butt through the hole and continued to let it live within our walls.

All life, no matter the perception of how grotesque it may be, is precious, and God placed it upon this earth to fulfill a purpose. This little mouse and my mother taught me a valuable lesson at the age of five, and it was that all life should be valued, especially if we believe it offers us nothing in return.

CHAPTER 7
POWER OF A SMILE

There is a power that lies within

a smile; it sparks a fire within,

creating the twinkle within an eye.

A smile has the power and ability to shift your current experience. The perfect example of experiencing the power that lies within a smile is smiling at a stranger. If your smile is reciprocated with a smile, you instantly feel a moment of pure and loving energy exude from that person. A smile can speak to you without you even being spoken to. When a stranger smiles back at you, your energy field instantly shifts, and suddenly you begin to see all the beauty and joy in your life and in the world. It instantly uplifts your vibration and your spirit. Your body has nothing else to do but respond, and respond it will, and in the most profound ways! Your body can communicate without the utterance of a single word. The divine moment when a stranger enters your life and gifts you with a spontaneous act of kindness in the form of a smile means much more than what meets the eye. It's a form of social acceptance, integration, an act of acknowledging your existence, and that is quite powerful in and of itself. That stranger will have made a powerful impact on your life, and he or she will forever be imprinted in your memory. You will never forget that person and the love he or she showed you on that fine day.

The gift of a smile can heal your temporary moment of suffering, if indeed you are experiencing some sort of discomfort at that given time or place. A smile that has been brought forth can heal and bring instantaneous joy, thus removing any sort of discomfort. In moments when I was feeling down, I have been smiled at by a stranger, and I felt like it was an angel speaking to me in the form of a sign, saying, "You are loved! Don't worry about a thing!"

Perfect strangers have made my day and my experience so much better because of their smile, and I speak from my heart of hearts when I say this. They have touched my life in the most glorious ways, just with the simple act of a smile. So this gift of a smile I give to you here and now, and I pray that you continuously pass it on to those who enter your experience. Your beautiful light and joyous energy are meant to be felt by all. After all, smiles are free and a wonderful gift to give.

Let's flip the poles of polarity.

The opposite of this scenario is if you smile at a stranger, and in return, he or she completely ignores your smile and kind gesture. This can cause a major inner conflict and lead to negative emotions and thoughts. It can also lead to the feeling of rejection, and it has the power to bring your high vibration to a lower-level frequency, but fear not, my dear one! This will only occur if you give it power and allow it to affect you and your emotions, thus potentially leading to physical responses. Keep this in mind, and don't feed that negative energy, because we all know it has absolutely nothing to do with you! They are experiencing some sort of inner conflict. So, never take it personally. If you do take it personally, it can suddenly cause you to disconnect from people, causing you to question yourself and your actions, and maybe bring you to the point of saying, "That's the last time I ever smile at a stranger!" I'll say it again: don't take it personally! You are a being of love, infinite light, and joy, and your intentions toward others are genuine and pure.

You may begin to assume that you are unworthy of being smiled at, or ask yourself, "Why should I put myself out there only to be rejected by others in return?" This is a fair question, but why not? You truly have nothing to lose except your pride and ego, and that dynamic duo doesn't serve you or your higher self anyway. Those who resist beauty in forms of kindness from a loving smile are hurting inside and probably thinking, *My life sucks! What is there to smile about?* or *Why is he or she so happy?* So they need our loving smile and positive energy even more. The more you practice this on strangers, the more you will begin to feel the beneficial effects and the power behind it.

Test it out and see for yourself what happens when you smile at a stranger.

Heal the world and touch souls, one interaction at a time. Smile at strangers with loving energy everywhere you go. Carry that loving light, that divine spark of intelligence, and project it out of every pore in your body. Start with your eyes. Fill them with love and warmth, causing people to feel an instantaneous sense of acceptance and adoration. This will carry on within the human being you have influenced, and it will be passed onto others they encounter, like a beautiful ripple.

It will instantly lift them up and bring forth a contagious sense of joy that is bound to spread like wildfire. It's like what happens at a coffee shop pass it on when suddenly you get a free coffee and you're like, "wait, what? OMG! How did that just happen!" It's kind of like that but ten times better!

CHAPTER 8
POWER OF EYES

Eyes are the window to the soul, the

divine key to the infinite gate that

allows others to enter and witness

the essence of our eternal being.

Your eyes can smile as well. You can feel, sense and see the difference between a genuine smile and a fake one. Try this for me. Look at yourself in the mirror and give yourself a fake smile, and then smile at yourself with all the love, joy, and happiness. Focus on your eyes while doing both exercises. Did you feel the difference? As my great-grandmother, Mary, would always say, "The proof is in the pudding!"

Let's chime in on the negative pole of the spectrum, shall we? It is important for you to understand that the power within your eyes can also be used for harm, and it's important that you don't give anyone the evil eye that is filled with jealous or envious energy. You want to stay as pure of heart as possible. If you have a jealous thought come upon you and look at someone with that energy, I want you to turn it off immediately and seek forgiveness from the divine and that person. I'm not asking you to run up to that person and say, "I'm sorry for giving you the evil eye just now," but rather, bless him or her and say sorry while looking at him or her. That person doesn't need to hear you; the most important thing is the energy field, and the projection upon another is transmuted into a positive vibration that you are solely responsible for. Remember, all our actions are being recorded and are seen by God and The Angels. This will also teach your conscious and subconscious mind not to continue that type of behavior. Reverse engineer your thought patterns and tendencies. We can all become envious of things we do not possess, but we all have amazing qualities, and they are all so different as we are all different and unique. So instead of being envious of others, you can focus on your beautiful qualities by honoring the gifts from God, and in return, magnifying and multiplying them by tenfold.

You must always try to operate at the highest vibrational levels of love. This way you can shield yourself from all negative vibrations that come from others. You must be a powerful, light being on this plane of existence and use your eyes and the intention behind them accordingly.

You can easily make someone fall in love with you by using the power of your eyes with thoughts of seduction behind them. Again, you must be extremely careful that you don't attract the wrong person, which more than likely you will since you are operating from a low-level vibration to obtain what you desire. Be assured, it will never last, and it will fall into the darkness from which it came, ending painfully and suddenly.

So again, use your power only for good. This way it does not create bad karma for you and those on the receiving end of your powerful, seductive gaze. You will be creating a reality in which their truth and desires were not able to come into play, since they didn't even have a chance, falling victim to your lust and making choices strictly from passions and not from reason. This will cause them to behave in certain ways that you have set into motion, which they will solely be reacting to. When lower vibrations are being used and brought forth between lovers, it can end up being extremely negative, causing harmful behaviors that the couple wouldn't normally say or do, thus causing you both harm in the end.

You never want anyone to fall in love with you for the wrong reasons, like lust. Lust is a form of power, yes. However, it is a low-level vibration that's solely bonded to earth, and we all want heavenly, ascended love from above.

Looks of love and looks of lust are very different. It is

the true intention that comes from the power within the being. What you are saying in your mind and in your heart will easily be transferred through the vibrations of your body since all are in tune and operating from the same system, systematically charging up all the frequencies that will come pouring out of you like a cosmic tidal wave that electrifies every cell in your being and the one on the receiving end of your thoughts. Your eyes are the windows to your soul and true intentions.

Here are some examples: "I just adore you" (comes from a pure, loving thought) versus "I want to fuck you" (which is a low-vibrational, lustful thought and word)—excuse my French. I want you to get a clear understanding.

There is a profound energy in what I've stated above, and making you aware is why I am here.

Chapter 9
Power of Touch

Healing can begin with

a compassionate hug or a

gentle wipe of a tear.

There is a divine power in the human touch, and it is an undeniable force to be felt. There are signals that can be sent, thus creating a sensation by the way you touch someone and vice versa. We send and receive signals. You have the power within your tiny finger to make someone's heartbeat race a hundred miles an hour. It pumps the blood flow throughout his or her entire body and better yet, to the exact place you desire the most. Again, be aware of the intention behind your touch and the emotion you set forth. Touch is a form of body language and the most ancient way to communicate with all life forms. It has been hardwired into us from birth, beginning with our mother's touch and caress, which is a high-value form of safety and comfort. My mother used to touch and caress my eyebrows and eyelashes as a child, which would immediately send me into a relaxed and peaceful state, instantly inducing a deep sleep, just like magic.

Our skin is the largest organ and measures about two meters if laid out flat! It is filled with tiny receptors (nerves), giving and receiving messages in the form of goosebumps and chills. Touching someone is one of the best ways of communication, and the energy behind your touch is what is profoundly felt. Touching adds so much to the overall human experience. It has the power to relieve us from stress and anxiety by calming and soothing our bodies, minds, and spirits. Touch has the most profound healing powers. Even a touch that lasts for a split second can have a profound and lasting effect on the recipient, soothing the psychological responses by enhancing endorphins to the brain and raising serotonin levels, eventually releasing much-needed joy. Ironically enough, the release of oxytocin in the brain from a slight caress, a touch of our hair, or a kiss on the mouth can cause our insides to go crazy, releasing all kinds of fluids. Women produce milk from this hormone, while men produce semen. Hugging and lovemaking also increase oxytocin levels, which is believed to be a strong bonding hormone. Research revealed that women who are hugged by their husbands are less stressed than others who are single.

Hugging a spiritually positive person can realign all your energies, enhancing positive alignment and creating a positive mood. This can create healing deep from within. Many people are placed on this earth for this divine purpose alone. Light workers and healers are indeed real people whose only wish is to be loving, kind, and compassionate and live in peace with their fellow man, woman, the earth, and all life that dwells upon it.

To live in total and complete harmony is to spread love and joy to those who seek it.

There have been many reported cases of healing throughout the centuries. Many were performed by our Lord and Savior, Jesus Christ, Mother Mary, and Saints who have been chosen by God to perform acts of miracles on earth. The anointed ones have delivered people from pain, suffering, illnesses, and immense internal suffering.

There is a holy woman by the name of Mata Amritanandamayi Devi. She is a Hindu woman who is referred to as "the hugging saint," revered as a physical and a spiritual healer by her followers. Throughout her life she has encountered and embraced an astonishing thirty-four million people. That's a lot of spiritual juice! Amma (her nickname) has miraculously transformed all sorts of human suffering by transferring her loving compassion to all whom she embraces. Throughout her life, she has dedicated herself to the healing of many of those in need, from the suffering of the poor to spiritual, mental, and physical suffering. She uplifts the spirit by uplifting the body since all are connected. The mind can only keep up with the body, and the body can only keep up with the mind, and the spirit is the link that holds both together in perfect harmony. Many people have claimed that she has healed their pain from a single touch and embrace. One of her quotes that is dearest to my heart is, "Be like the honeybee who gathers only nectar where it goes. Seek the goodness found in everyone."

Let's flip the poles of polarity once more. Negative energy can be felt through touch as well, causing extreme forms of discomforts: stress, anxieties, and fear. When people are going through a tough time, they can transfer their negative emotions and vibrations by a simple touch if you are not aware of it and have your spiritual shield up to block it. This is called energy transfer. When you are hugged or touched by an individual who is spiritually conflicted by depression, for example, it can cause you harm. The negative energy can leave its residue on you. It is important for you to be spiritually strong and aware that these energies do exist out in the world and dwell among people. It is important to be extremely careful when choosing someone to hug or allowing them to even lay a finger on you. A hug from a stranger is risky business. So choose wisely on who you let into your sacred space.

In truth, you don't even have to make physical contact for negative energy to be felt by the recipient. There is an energy field that emanates from the point of your finger. In many cultures around the world, it is believed to be bad manners to point at someone. Have you ever pointed at someone or been pointed at? You instantly feel strange and uncomfortable. This action toward you is then followed by a question: "Why is this person pointing at me?" Generally, it's a negative vibration coming from the intent of that person that can be felt five hundred feet away. Yes, vibrations are that powerful. That power is within us all. So, think next time you point at someone.

God and his Holy Angels watch over everything we do. No matter what is going on in our daily lives, it's important to know that we are never alone. Please remember to be a person of loving-kindness even to those who persecute you. It has everything to do with them and nothing to do with you.

CHAPTER 10
POWER OF INTENTION

Every word, thought, and action

has an intention behind it.

The true definition of intention via Google "is a thing invented; an aim or plan."

The power of intention is the initiating force that carries out your thoughts and actions in your day-to-day life. Stating your intentions plays a key role in manifesting your aspirations. In return, your intended reality magically comes to fruition. Holding on to your intentions by thought will automatically be followed by a projected mental image of what that intention entails. This enhances the vibration of your intention until it becomes a reality. Your mind is powerful and will effortlessly place the intention (image) into your mind, thus creating future memories. There you will live out the experience and create emotional responses as if you are living it. You will feel the joy, satisfaction, and excitement. By the simple act of playing out your manifestations through thought, you will create the vibration as if it is attainable, which it is.

You can do anything if you put your mind to it! There is so much hidden wisdom in this saying, and once we unlock the hidden codes in this universe, we began to understand the process it is made of, and all that is hidden will be revealed.

Vocalizing your intentions is the key to opening Pandora's box of endless possibilities for your life and what you wish to accomplish. Everything has a vibration, especially your intentions.

When you wake from a deep sleep and the sun is radiating into your room, filling it with light and ethereal energy, plant the seed of your intention. Continually plant the seed of your intention throughout your day. The more the merrier. The more you water it, the more it will grow. You will start the transmutation process of your life experiences since you will have your eye on the prize.

Begin your day with your set intention in mind and what you wish to accomplish. Set various goals. Here's one example: My intention is to have patience while I am working with clients today. The key word is *intention*. The effects are undeniable.

When you choose the word *want* or *need* instead, those words contain a different vibration, and you can sense it right away. Wanting something means, to the subconscious mind, that you are "without" when in fact you are in abundance and constantly creating new paths in your life with the power to lead you in various directions.

Repeat after me: "I want to be an honest person." How does that resonate? What feelings and thoughts came to the forefront of your mind? What images were displayed in your conscious and subconscious mind?

When you use the word *want*, it's truly a low vibration as well as the phrase, "I want."

Now, again, repeat after me: "I desire to be an honest person." Remember to pay attention to the emotions and imagery that came forth, and take as much time as you need to place the vibration it brings.

When you use the word *desire*, you can feel a certain energy exude from the sacral center, especially if you're more feminine than masculine. This power word has a lot of juice and cosmic pull. However, beware of the way you use it and of the situation. It's a word that can bring sexual energy and can be used to seduce your intended outcome.

Now say, "I intend on being an honest person." Can you feel that vibration and what that specific word does? You are basically creating a future experience. You're shouting out to the heavens that your purpose is to be honest and you are manifesting the power within that word.

Someone very special to me once said, "You can tell a lot about a person by the words they speak."

There is a beautiful truth behind that phrase. We all need to be aware of the things we say and the vibrations and intentions behind them.

When you use the word *intend*, you are saying to God and the universe that you are a person of integrity and driven by purpose, and you will be rewarded for such ethereal behaviors.

When you place your intention into the universe, you are planting a cosmic seed, sprung up from the conscious and subconscious mind. Since your true intention comes from a longing to fulfill your life's true purpose, if that is to obtain infinite peace or pure abundance, it's only for you to truly know. Only your higher self has the awareness and knowledge of what that purpose is. The more in tune you are with God and your higher self, the more wisdom you will attain and apply on this educational journey we call life.

Manifesting your intended outcome will bring you so much joy, and to know that God is listening and working in your favor is the most exciting part of it all.

Stay in the light, and stay in the essence of love forever more. May God and his holy angels continue to watch over you.

I'm hopeful that this spiritual journey has enhanced your life, raised your vibrations, and far exceeded any expectations.

May you continue to be blessed and live in gratitude by praising God every day.

Be in a state of self-awareness so you may become a better version of yourself.

Activate your higher state of being, and make your spiritual ideas physical realities. Do this by the power of God, with God, and for God, always and forever.

Printed and bound by PG in the USA

USA20199PGIL